YOUR KNOWLEDGE HAS VALUE

- We will publish your bachelor's and master's thesis, essays and papers

- Your own eBook and book - sold worldwide in all relevant shops

- Earn money with each sale

Upload your text at www.GRIN.com
and publish for free

Pat Roupin

Is participative innovation encouraging social entrepreneurship?

GRIN Publishing

Bibliographic information published by the German National Library:

The German National Library lists this publication in the National Bibliography; detailed bibliographic data are available on the Internet at http://dnb.dnb.de .

Imprint:

Copyright © 2013 GRIN Verlag GmbH
Print and binding: Books on Demand GmbH, Norderstedt Germany
ISBN: 978-3-656-92175-2

This book at GRIN:

http://www.grin.com/en/e-book/294177/is-participative-innovation-encouraging-social-entrepreneurship

Is participative innovation encouraging social entrepreneurship?

Keywords: Co-creation, Design Thinking, Business, Innovation, Social entrepreneurship, Cybernetics, crowdsourcing, Complexity

Patrick Roupin

Introduction

For nearly a century creativity has been understood as a key ingredient of business creation across thousands of design who took shape as product, service, solution and social planning. Participative innovation comes with a new set of values to reinforce the creative potential of organisation. Participative innovation is ether understood as an internal phenomenon of organisation or a manifestation which is happening outside the boundary of the corporate structure. Initially we would have a look to both the aspects. In house participative innovation refers to the fact that workers and managers associate to create new business models and solutions for the consumers. We call participative innovation the point that the workers who are involved in the creative process are not supposed to be in charge of innovation contribution. Participative innovation implies that an organisation would have adopted a politic of democratization of the creative process across its managerial layers to leverage new business opportunities. For the past 3 decades, participative innovation has grown significantly. The company Google who institutionalized this value, made it mandatory to workers to involve themselves in prospective projects a certain amount of time from their schedule. It is believed that number of Google innovation came from this initiative. Giving workers some freedom to problem solving in the ever fragmented industry leads companies to new areas of business development. Today, there is a common acceptance that participative innovation is promising. More recently participative innovation has got a new sense by including public and user participation. Participative innovation advocates the importance of including the user on the conceptualisation of product, service and policy. This second aspect of participative innovation interest us more particularly has it may lead to social entrepreneurship which is the objective of the research question that would be developed in this proposal.

To demonstrate the potential of participative innovation I shall dress a parallel with design thinking that is most of the time a non-inclusive discipline. Bruce Nussebaum has demonstrated that failure in design thinking is due to monopolistic approach by most companies and political groups towards the society with regards to value creation. Rather than wanting to "change the world" through design thinking and business it should be like society leaders support people in making the world as they want using participative innovation. In short, it is questioned that shifting the power of design thinking from the designer's hand to the common man's hand could lead to a more effective way of producing innovation. In this research I try to demonstrate that social changes lead people to be increasingly reactive to systems and solutions presented to them. We witness a re-appropriation of the industry, the politic and the social.

 At the lecture of sociological concepts of identity, and essays from notorious designers, philosopher and business mam we assume that our economy could be at the beginning of a new economic order that would give power to consumer as a democratic necessity to balance the corporate lobby. This approach sometimes referred as *'prosumerism'* would radically transform the purpose of design in the corporate environment. It is therefore believed that corporate would be re-elected to the role of social enabler rather that been the creative think-tank of the consumerist society has it has been the case since the Second World War. However, participative innovation leads to large questioning in time of economic recession and environmental instability. Participation is negatively associated to *"working for free"* with concerns in terms of intellectual properties. Today's businesses are facing the issue of associating with the consumer through participative innovation while maintaining a climate of fair exchange.

By stimulating participative innovation business and society put themselves at risk that a large part of the creative potential slip from their hands and get developed by third party individuals and organization. However participative innovation requires the nest of a cybernetic environment for business development what make it mandatory for businesses to concede part of its intellectual production. As Prahalad and Krishnan mention in the New Age of Innovation; ""No firm is big enough in scope and size to satisfy the experiences of one single consumer" and that is the whole challenge of a participative innovation approach. User requirement get so fragmented that no business can have the capacity of responding to all the facet of the consumer experience. This statement also implies that ultimately, firms would depend on individual and/or start-up to generate the value necessary to respond to the needs of unique consumers. This, take us to the purpose of this research:

Is participative innovation encouraging social entrepreneurship?

In this research proposal we try to demonstrate the various mechanism that lead citizens and consumers to take initiatives towards social, economic and commercial causes. We show how this relationship can be productive as well as destructive for organisations. Finally we analyse if there is a causal effect of participative innovation towards social entrepreneurship.

Existing research

Research covered in this section cover 4 principal aspect of the initial research question that would be elaborated in large. Here is a short introduction:

1. **Identity:** Contemporary individuals are moving from a social role model to a much individualistic approach of their self-perception. It implies major changes in terms of social behaviour and the place and role of individuals in society.
2. **Technology:** The universe of technology is increasingly cybernetic increasing the range of possibilities of product and service development. We explore technological possibilities in the global economy.
3. **Design:** The traditional User Centric Design theory remains at the hearth of product and service development. However numbers of signs are showing that *"designers know nothing and users everything"*. We explore the notion of co-creation and democratic innovation.
4. **Socioeconomic:** The fall of identity and institutional identity is a direct consequence of people self-determination and entrepreneurship in the contemporary society. We analyse how organizations are bound to embrace democratic innovation.

The reader may find difficulties in relating the points that have been introduced. However it should be understood that this diversity reflects the complexity of today's business situation. Business environment is increasingly complex; managers need to embrace this complexity with new values and new analytical skills. What follow should be read as an essays with lots of subjectivity. What we are trying to do here is not to affirm the existence of such ecosystem but draw the line of a hypothetical work frame.

Identity

Been from industrial design background it is my concern to put de user at the centre of my analysis. In the context of co-creation the problematic of understanding the user is even more important that we are expecting from the user to reveal his or her creative potential. This implies that the user should be in a mood of creation. Identity and creation have a strong link on which the user reveal his potential and reinvent his own identity. It is not surprising that the emergence "identity crisis" in the contemporary society goes along with the emergence of the democratization of the creative process. In their quest for freedom contemporary individuals are bond to constantly reinvent themselves through various means of creation.

The profile of contemporary individuals

From a sociologic perspective, Professor Jacques Paitra announced in 2000 the raise of the "society of autonomy". He depicts a modern society on which individual tempts to gain autonomy and become vibrant social players, by taking initiative of all kind to fitful their passion and aspiration. With the raise of social networking Paitra's prediction has never been so truthful. Any individual in the world today can manage his social network at the finger touch connect with their pairs and create vibrant projects. That new social construction is impacting politics, social and economy trends.

The definition of "Self" is continuously involving and studied by anthropologist, sociologist and philosopher to the benefits of corporate and society leader. The University of Toronto promote extensive research with regard to the hybridity of the contemporary culture. "Hybridity, neither stranger nor familiar" was the name of an international research project they conducted in 2010.

The amount of research dedicated to the theory of self are still limited and mostly explorative. Here is a personal finding I have been using for the past 6 years to justify my research methods in several projects.

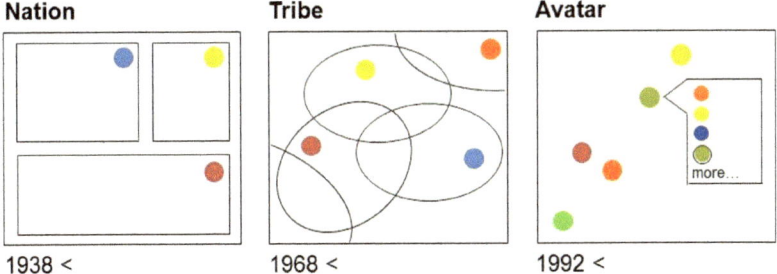

Self-identity involve with the development of technologies and society. Here is a chronology of 'self' identification moving from Nation to Tribe and then Avatar from 1938 till date. It may be representative of the evolution of "self" in the contemporary culture.

Nation: Individuals identify themselves with respect to their culture, religion and nation. The boundary of identification is clear and structured. I associate the date of 1938 to the creation of the Volkswagen Coccinelle by Ferdinand Porsche who represents le National-Socialism of Hitler. The notion of 'Self' is therefore associate to the nation, its code and artefacts.

Tribe: As globalisation took place the term *"tribe"* were extensively used to describe connected individuals across the globe who share the same values regardless their nation and culture. The boundary of identification is fuzzy by nature since people come from diversified cultural background to embrace new code and value. The date of 1968 refers to the social revolution during which traditional values have been questioned. The hippie formed communities with new ideal of society. The notion of community identification still remains important.

Avatar: As people get extensively exposed to hybrid identity, the self-identification grown rapidly and deeply. This is accentuated by the culture of autonomy described by Paitra. The *"Generation Z"* requires instant way of responding to identity issues and temps to fall into *"Avatar"* identity. The avatar is a unique individual who change his identity and the way he present himself instantly with regard to environment and life situation. Initially popularized by video games, the avatar culture takes all segment of the society with a multitude of possibilities individuals can switch from in real world as well. The avatar culture is bound to grow as geo-cultural distances continue to collapse. I retain the date of 1992 for the emergence of the Avatar culture; it is the birth of Internet for the general public and the beginning of 3D video games with avatar. Gamers have an active role on the world they project themselves. Similarly the internet becomes a virtual universe of signs that make sense to the user leading him in re-shaping his own identity.

We are now 20 years, from the beginning of the Avatar culture. Since 2012, The MTV Show – Catfish initiated by Nev Schulman beautifully present American people leading several fake identities over the internet for years. It is not rare to find people today who have no social connection with their surrounding and an active social life with the virtual world. They may keep their real identity or been 'catfish' (fake identity). The fact is that people find online values that may not be available in their physical neighbourhood. Without falling in the extreme of fake identity, the catfish phenomenon is representative of changes in society. People are more likely to lead an isolated identity within the hyper connected world on which they find repairs more that in reality. The development of ecommerce also encourages people in reaching niche markets that respond to their personal aspiration.

Globalisation both merges and singularises individuals in a contradictive effort. This complexity of *"self"* identification is on the heart of every individual and is one of the greatest challenges for the future of design.

Consumer identity crisis and market trends

Responding to consumer identity has always been the concern of artists, designers and trendsetters who served the industry with creative insights since its very beginning. Artist and designer had the prestigious social status of sensing what is *"in"* and more or less impose it to the rest of the world. In the past decade the limitation between *"consumer"* and *"producer"* roles have been blurred due to the tendency of many consumers in setting what is *"in"* and by the way turning the pyramid culture ups and down. Individuals from all walks of life have been stealing the audience that were before reserved to a very limited class of privileged who were setting the tone. The media industry is probably the most spectacular demonstration of the ups and down of the information flow. This industry has been metamorphosed by entrepreneur journalist of all kind. The development of blogs, social network and unstructured reporting, disassembled the news and media industry thus forcing it to move from the print to digital format with more targeted content. The entertainment and musical industry had to run competition with Google, YouTube, Torrent and other video sites to give the chance for everyone to become a user and a creator. Those very few examples prove that content and creation become accessible to all and the world is getting empowered not by creative institution but people who individually create with different level of professionalism. How long would it take for a typical household to become a micro-industry who create replicate and network values of all kinds. Technologies like 3D printing are on the way of democratisation. It gives a chance to contemporary artisan to manufacture their creations without complex outsource. Today lots of people convert their passion into livelihood through the internet. As the rate of unemployment continues to grow, people will continue searching alternatives to the streamline economy. Small scale initiative have the advantage of been socially integrated, flexible and highly personal which allow closeness to the needs of targeted market segmentation. Business and society have the interest in encouraging people in their endeavour of value creation; by providing business platforms to streamline their interest into economic reality. Another factor that could be responsible for the fracture between design thinking and participative innovation is the dismantlement of social boundaries and cultures. The Internet has so fractured us (people) globally that we no longer are looking for mass-culture experiences earlier provided by public leaders and international brands. The internet is a kaleidoscope of colour, design and lifestyle experience which has become the common's man culture. The best stand next to the worst, the real next to the unreal, and the truth next to the false. It is an incredible cacophony on which none would find a clue to assess what is right to go with.

"In the old days, style used to be the prerogatives of a small group of people. Now it is a national sport. Ticket sales are exploding. People are pouring into the arena in such vast numbers that none of us can keep track of the rule book. Et voila! Nobody is keeping score. All bets are off. Anything goes."

Simon Doonan creative director at Barneys upscale 2010

The notion of style or design is not restricted to physical artefact but from a much holistic perspective to the complete ecosystem that surround the usage of a product, system or social organisation. Product and system of all kind are charged of historic, philosophic and anthropologic insights that all together describe people's art of living. As design was made for specific social trends belonging to specific culture and nation; things were simple. Product, system and solution were made for a specific scenario. Today's consumers are so versatile that design is thrown to an extremely wide range of socio-types, who at one particular point of time are receptive to specific design. Sizing market and assess leading consumer segment behaviour become near to impossible. Marketing scholar call it the *'Generation Z'*, a generation who's filiation is in constant evolution. In this context no companies, politic, artist or brand would ever find the strength to re-generate the mass culture movement of the past. New tools and technologies are needed to empower consumers in their search of satisfaction.

'The most important thing to understand is that the modern individual is sentenced to work building sense of what makes sense to him. It is in this sense that we can speak of totalitarian identity construction: it has to build a full, obvious, it closes all the gaps in order to be fluid, efficient ... Always fight for recognition against the background of mental fatigue, tired of being oneself'

Kaufmann, 2004 (Google Translation from French)

Contemporary individuals are in need of forging new social identity to face the individualistic world they have created. Kaufmann demonstrates today's environment as *'totalitarian'* with regards to the necessity for contemporary individuals in constantly re-shaping their identity. Kaufman also demonstrates how this search for identity is often converted into consumerism.

Technology

Today's society face huge disruption caused by the spread of social media technologies, the urbanization of the planet, the rise and fall of nations, global warming, and overpopulation. The continuation of consumerism and the way we encourage consumerism through design thinking is questioned; a large portion of the design community aims for a new relationship between design and society.

Several alternatives to consumerism have been advanced with more or less of success. One retain my attention particularly is the concept of crowdsourcing revealed by Jeff Howe who advocate that the power of the crowd is driving the future of business. Howe present hundreds of case studies on which the crowd has been determining to the drive of business. Howe does not only defend crowdsourcing as a mono-directional relationship from crowd to business. He present crowdsourcing as a bipolar relationship on which people and business create new arena of development for the benefit of both ends.

Howe was one of the first scholars to use the term *"prosumerism'* to define the relationship between people and business in the process of co-creation. *"prosumerism'* could be understood as an advanced form of participative innovation with the plus of entrepreneurship Howe, believe in the power of consumers and their ability to craft tomorrow's industry. Technology is responsible for the democratization of information in terms of viewing as well as creation.

"Since 2008 the number of things connected to the internet exceeds the number of people. By 2020 they will be 50 billion of things connected to the internet. By 2012, 20 typical households will generate more traffic than the entire internet in 2008" - Source Cisco

Design

The efficiency of design thinking has been criticized by scholars in business reality. As practitioner I am the first sceptical with regard to the efficiency of design thinking to produce realistic business model and solutions. As it is advocated by Professor Bruce Nussebaum; I do not believe in design thinking as a managerial tool to create new business but as a tool to develop creative leader's culture". It empowers designers and business leaders providing them a larger outlook to problem solving and business creation. Nussebaum continue with the idea that business benefit from design thinking is low; but the contributions of design thinking to the field of design and to society at large are immense. Design thinking has diverted designers and the power of design from a focus artefact and narrow consumerist aesthetics marketplace to the much wider social space of systems and society.

In the present ecosystem of innovation, design thinking is used by business and society leaders to create values to consumer market.

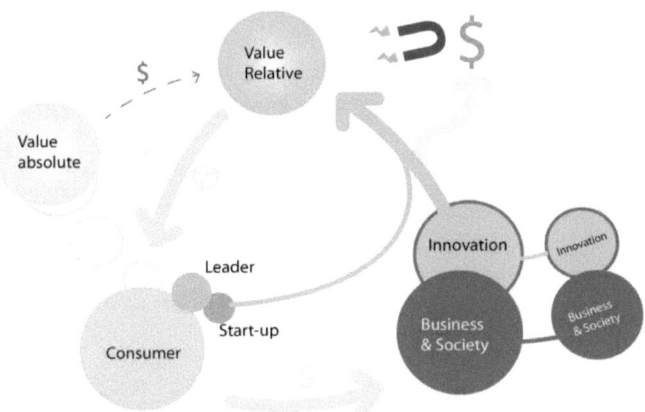

The consumer, leader and start-up have a very limited possibility of creating, developing and implementing values for the consumer market. They have a passive role as consumer. Values are drained into standard offerings to gather the need of large consumer segment. Values absolute cheers to individual are neglected as they cannot be turned into business; the consumer is bound to compromise from what is cheer to him and what is available in the market. In todays over saturated market added to sustainable issues and economic meltdown I like to think that this model of creating, producing and consuming will change.

Design thinking moving towards an integrative approach of consumption

In spite of a well-organized design thinking strategy projects often goes to failure due to unpredicted user resistance that cannot be accessed by stakeholders. This fact is commonly accepted by a large majority of design firms in every vertical of the industry. Scholars have been advocating the importance of accepting and celebrating failure in the corporate world to rebound with success. Encourage people in taking risk seems to be a positive change however the possibility of exploration would continue to increase has the mass consumer market dismantle. Keeping track of success and failure would become irrelevant considering the unique character of each business cases. User resistance factors are increasingly volatile and cluttered.

The three factors that would make business exploration and assessment increasingly complex and expensive are:

- The end of mass consumption and mass culture.

- The spread of specific technological solutions at every end of industry.

- The development of emerging markets that would grow the overall amount of consumers and form new clusters.

In that context; corporate companies are required to make a large amount of live test projects, required to equips themselves with assessment processes and develop generic business development solutions. This ecosystem would require a symbiotic relationship between consumer and producer which clearly announce the era of participative innovation.

Design thinking as a process and approach to problem is no more the privilege of large corporates but a revolution which will be self-generated at social level. The social revolution by design has to be framed and encourage by corporate and society for the benefit of the world economy. Business and society leaders need to adapt to a *'prosumer'* approach of business; become facilitator of change rather than change maker.

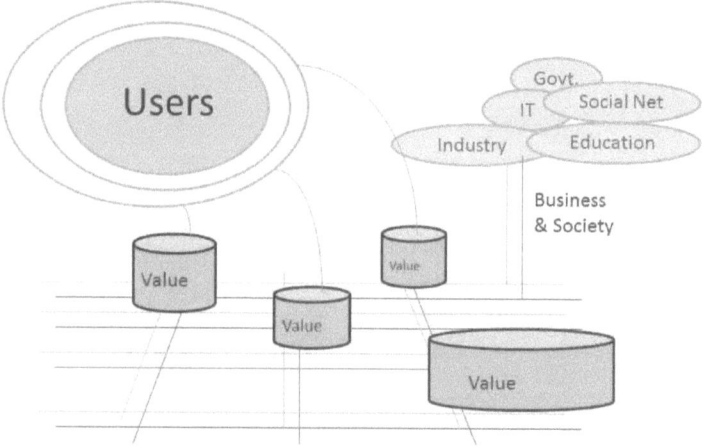

Many companies have already demonstrated that it is possible to align our deep aspiration as human being with efficient market offer and profit generation in a single goal. However rare are those companies who broke the traditional frameworks of producer to consumer.

In the future ecosystem above presented, values will be generated and self-sustained by people and communities. Business and society will be providing tools, process and solutions to encourage individual and community initiatives. 'Avatar' individuals may want to associate with a multitude of projects that cheer to them and bring their insights and values to the project. The fact that business ventures are built over personal inspiration in a co-creative environment ensure the interest for the project. Thanks to crowdsourcing we have tools to assess the on-going viability of a business rather than relying on stakeholders' subjective opinion. Individual projects may be connected to larger networking projects under an umbrella of self-learning solution.

In the ideal economy **Value Absolute, Value Relative** and **Profit** would be aligned as a single goal for people, business and society.

They will be 3 groups of players in the making of values:

Consumer may want to associate with a particular ecosystem and benefit from it simply as consumer. They are likely to share values generated by the group project as we share values with brands today. The environment provided will invite a few to move from the consumer group towards the leader.

Leader who masteries the values shared by the group. They are passionate, specialist, self-motivated, guru, scientist, researcher, etc. They have the leadership profile to involves other into their cause and generate the interest of the general public.

Start-up converts value generation into business venture with the support of business and society leaders. They create the link between the industry and the leader to manufacture, edit and implement solutions.

Business & Society would increasingly become omnipresent and support individuals in their own walk of value creation without interfering. Their role is not to generate changes but to facilitate change in society by providing the platform for business.

A democratic approach of innovation accessible to all not in term of consumption but production; which has rightly given the birth to the portmanteau word *'prosumerism'*. Participative innovation associated to social entrepreneurship could its definition.

Socioeconomic

Sustainable development has often been presented as a way to limit our impact on the environment. Rare are those who envisage sustainable development as a potential to generate new business solution. Holmgren's sustainable development philosophy applied to design can not only eliminate user resistance to change but also generate new aspirations.

A parallel can be made between the modern intensive agriculture which to some extent is going against the nature and yet experimental methods like permaculture work in symbioses with nature. The modern agriculture extracts from nature the best of it as a slave whose desire for growth and aspiration are not respected.

Similarly, in the consumer economy people are enslaved with marketing aspiration; they are requested to burn goods in surplus. Designers attach themselves to create new needs that sometimes work against people's nature. I see it as an exploitation of human vulnerability to pertain consumerism; thus it may sound as an effective capitalist ecosystem, it has its own limit fixed by human resistance. The question is not about questioning the legitimacy of capitalism but rather the way it drives its own purpose.

"Our enormously productive economy demands that we make consumption our way of life, that we convert the buying and use of goods into rituals, that we seek our spiritual satisfaction and our ego satisfaction in consumption. We need things consumed, burned up, worn out, replaced and discarded at an ever-increasing rate"

Victor Lebow, Economist 1955

If we now take a framework which is more durable and respectful of the human nature we could see the emergence of Humanistic Design as announced by Bruce Nussebaum. Humanistic Design could be the emergence of a design philosophy that work in symbiosis with human potential, desires and aspiration for growth. People's aim for prosperity is a never ending source of wealth creation for economy. Empowering the society with creative thinking could be the next big step of design.

The new programs in Social Innovation at Parsons, School of Visual Arts, Stanford and Columbia, are signs that the society itself is a source of innovation and growth for businesses. That's people; common man can themselves become the initiator of large social venture with thunderous return for business and society.

In the following tables we analyse how moving from a consumerist model of society to a social entrepreneurial model would generate new business opportunities while contributing to the resolution of some major social issues.

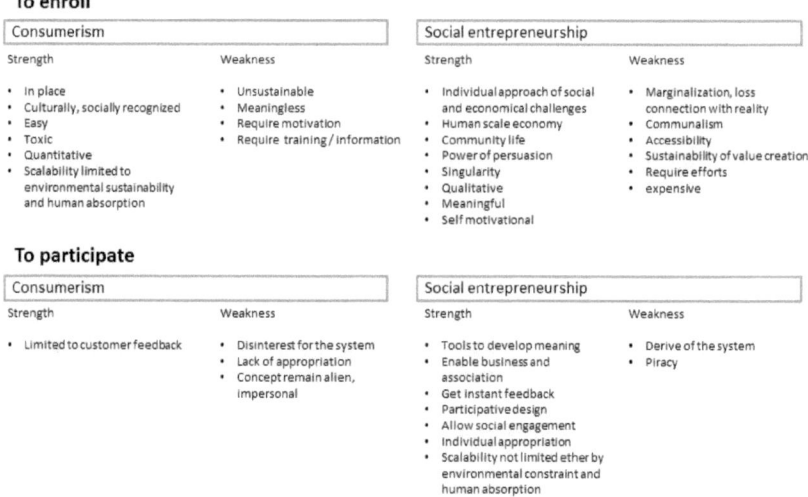

To enroll

Consumerism		Social entrepreneurship	
Strength	Weakness	Strength	Weakness
• In place • Culturally, socially recognized • Easy • Toxic • Quantitative • Scalability limited to environmental sustainability and human absorption	• Unsustainable • Meaningless • Require motivation • Require training / information	• Individual approach of social and economical challenges • Human scale economy • Community life • Power of persuasion • Singularity • Qualitative • Meaningful • Self motivational	• Marginalization, loss connection with reality • Communalism • Accessibility • Sustainability of value creation • Require efforts • expensive

To participate

Consumerism		Social entrepreneurship	
Strength	Weakness	Strength	Weakness
• Limited to customer feedback	• Disinterest for the system • Lack of appropriation • Concept remain alien, impersonal	• Tools to develop meaning • Enable business and association • Get instant feedback • Participative design • Allow social engagement • Individual appropriation • Scalability not limited ether by environmental constraint and human absorption	• Derive of the system • Piracy

Enrolling in consumerism like enrolling into social entrepreneurship would have some strength and weakness for the consumers who are also citizen and eventually social entrepreneur. This table offer an overview about how moving from one model to other one would generate new opportunities and conflicts. This list is non exhaustive and hypothetical, it provides actionable insight to develop research question and argumentation.

Research Question

Is participative innovation encouraging social entrepreneurship?

Castiaux and Paque describe participative innovation has a discipline that conciliate innovation and quality management. The discipline is organized in such way that various group and stakeholders can participate to the process within the corporate boundary. The challenge in this case maybe to interpret participative innovation in a more holistic way that includes the general public and not only the firm stakeholders.

Encouraging in this context may refer to any form of open space left over the practice of participative innovation. Encouragement may include but are not limited to a form of social reword, financial gain or personal accomplishment.

The distinction between business entrepreneurship and social entrepreneurship is that the first one measure performance with financial gain. The second may also refer to financial gain to asses performance but broaden their goal towards social, cultural, and environmental objectives. Austin, Stevenson and Wei-Skillern stress the number of similarity and challenges between both the types of ventures and the possible means of moving from one model to the other. This research aims to study both the aspects of entrepreneurship and social entrepreneurship while revealing the risk and opportunities a falling either on one or another category with regard to its impact on active participation from innovation perspective.

Academic and managerial relevance

Participative innovation has already shown its influence in the setting of co-creative design function. Now, there is a new paradigm under the co-creative inclusion of consumers. The possibility of this evolution has been demonstrated through this research proposal. I invite the reader to be sceptical with regard to the business opportunities engaged by participative innovation. However, and it is the counterpart of this hypothesis, I believe there is strong risk that any involvement into participative innovation would lead to an ever meet interest of the general public for social entrepreneurship. This would drastically change the role of corporation in the long term. Participative innovation and social entrepreneurship are two concepts who have a strong interlink. Considering the first one without envisaging the risk of been captured by the second one is a managerial challenge that requires investigation.

Individual consumers have several levels of involvement in the process of participative innovation. Most advanced theories of participative innovation imply a culture of innovation implemented at multi-level within the organization or outside the organization. This concept is referred as dyade or triade of innovation. A dyade include managers and workers in the process of value creation. Whereas a triade include managers, works but also consumers in the process of value creation. Organization like *Ikea* try to move from a dyade to a triad model by outsourcing their work to consumers; including their creative work however their core business model is still middle-of-the-road a dyade on which managers and workers elaborates a commercial offer addressed to the consumer. For organization like *Facebook* that notion of consumer/contributor has been a base for their business model which is a triade. Just ask yourself the question. What would be *Facebook* without user's contribution? The answers would be close to nothing. We may conclude that consumer's involvement is less for a brand like *Ikea* than *Facebook*.

In this hypothetical scenario we try to demonstrate that many companies are at the verge of getting customers to pay for their work. And that extensively consumer wants and/or are forced to produce values as a joint effort between business and consumer. This assumption, if true, breaks all known ideas about consumer/user centric development and targeted marketing. Moreover it questions the role of managers, workers and consumers within and outside the organization. The raise of consumer's involvement in the process of value creation reveals plenty of challenges in terms of organization behavior.

In this hypothetical scenario we are pushing the role of consumer at the extreme of what it could be in term of consumer involvement. The consumer is not only an opinion leader; it also has a role of leadership and business developer.

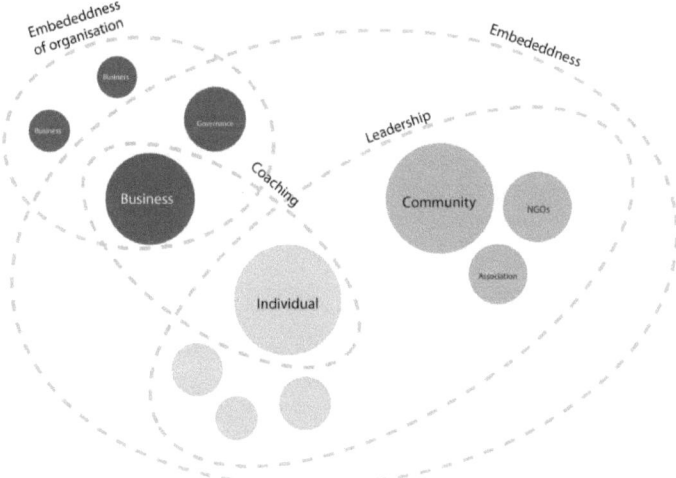

The reader would rightly be skeptical about this hypothetical ecosystem of organization behavior though the organizational structure of the previous mentioned example *Facebook* may not be fare from the present hypothesis.

In this hypothetical ecosystem we identified 4 fields of research for organization behavior:

- Leadership
- Coaching
- Embededdness
- Embededdness of organization & Industry categorization

We assume that equal attention to those corposants is the structure that allows businesses to stimulate participative innovation. We understand that working on those corposants allow organizations to move towards an effective managerial change.

Embededdness

As per Wikipedia embededdness refer to *"the degree to which economic activity is constrained by non-economic institutions."* The word *"constraint"* seems to be important with regard to the economic model we are studying. *"Constraint"* is negatively associated to the barriers businesses face in the development of their activity. Cannot this barrier be an opportunity for businesses to respond to social challenges?

Today's businesses are threatened by the public opinion for not playing their role in society. Poverty, global warming and economic austerity are among the reproaches given to corporation by the general public. Participative innovation is surely one of the way businesses can stimulate to reinforce their social message and position themselves as a change maker. An economy based on co-creation, participative innovation and social entrepreneurship would ultimately raise new challenges in terms of right, law and policy. Considering people as *"consumers"* is legally less engaging that considering them as *"co-creator"* even more business partners. What we try to demonstrate here is that a society that has inclination towards participative innovation temps to encourage embededdness between its protagonist that are the business, its consumer/producer and the governance. Moreover that social entrepreneurship has a strong tendency of sharing values with mon-business representatives as such as NGO and association whose aims is mainly towards social empowerment.

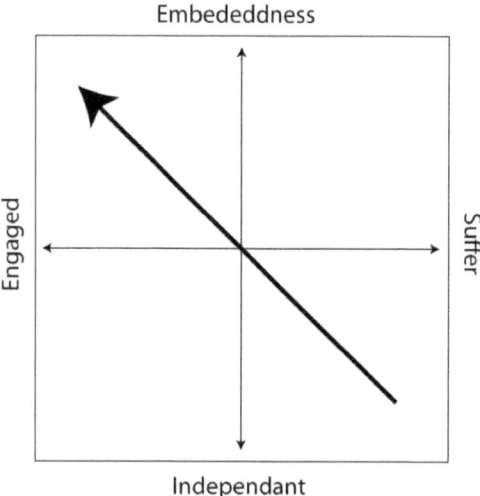

As a reasonable projection we can assume that businesses would move towards a stronger embededdness that would be *'Engaged"* and not *"Suffer"* like before. Engaged embededdness is about business commitment towards the society to generate social values as politic of sustainability. Democratic innovation, participative innovation, co-creation and social entrepreneurship are means of social empowerment and wealth creation however it would also temps to reinforce businesses embededdness in the following domain:

- Structural
- Cognitive
- Cultural
- Politic
- Economic
- Technologic
- Religious / Philosophic

The concept of participative innovation and social entrepreneurship is by definition a collective act that would take its source in society's culture and history. Charged of collective emotional meaning participative innovation won't be an alien proposition of the industry towards the society but a co-produced model between business and society. That co-production requires understanding and vision sharing between both business and society to create the environment platform appropriate to creative participation. We will be using the classification Luhmann to understand the impact of participative innovation and entrepreneurship on the different function of the society. We will classify insight by social function and hope to find a theoretical model that applies to all co-created systems of society.

Coaching & Leadership

Initial research let us understand that the transition from participative innovation to social entrepreneurship would take place at individual level. The individual get motivated ether by the desire of social recognition, financial gain or simply by the challenge of entrepreneurship. Therefore, the *"idea"* become a business opportunity individual which to carry as value proposition towards the community. Regardless the fact that the "idea" could be the fruit of an individual or collective work; at this particular point, someone would need to take the lead of bringing this idea to a higher level of conceptualisation. Caring this "idea" towards the community require motivation and leadership from the candidate to generate motivation around the proposition. It requires motivation from the individual but also support from the organisation that engage into participative behaviour. We refer this support to the co-creative leader as *"coaching"*. We assume that organisation that support participative innovation have a politic of *"coaching"* towards co-creative leaders that maybe user, consumer or workers.

From the organisation perspective, coaching on the right direction reveal 4 main defies:

- Recognize the input of the *"co-creator"*, understand the participative innovation contributor.
- Develop the necessary adjustments for its development as innovation champion.
- Train employees on the appropriate changes to accommodate the needs to the new idea.
- Win the support of the employees with the persuasiveness of the appropriate adjustments.

However, co-creative contributors would have to be understood independently with consideration to their individual social environment. Here comes psychology to bring light on how individuals take decisions to migrate from participation to entrepreneurship behaviour. We aims to prove the relationship between participative innovation and social entrepreneurship, later demonstrate academically how the behavioural change take place from on state to the other.

Industry categorization & embededdness of organizations

Prahalad and Krishnan have been advocating a new approach of innovation based on the association of business supply chain they named N=1 and R=G. They started from the simple idea that rather than having a single company supplying millions of consumers they would be many company associating to supply a single consumer. Yes, you read it well, Prahalad and Krishnan want to address to single consumer across the globe with a truly personalized offer. The concept seems to be counterproductive and again all logic of mass consumption. But let compare this logic to the previous example, Facebook - Among the 1 billion Facebook users; are they 2 Facebook users who have the same Facebook page? Not. Facebook may propose hundreds of applications; the way users associate those applications together and connect it to their social experience is unique. Every Facebook user has a *"unique"* layout of the social platform, not yet a *"personalized"* experience. The nuance is critical. N = 1 is about "personalized, co-creation of experiences"--not mass customization or a customer of one. Facebook like many other companies are on the way to convert their business model into a truly N=1, R=G offer. yet the shift is critical and require consumer participation.

Prahalad and Krishnan, co-created personal experience is name N=1 and R=G. It propose a business remodelling as following.

1 business to mass consumer   mass business to 1 consumer

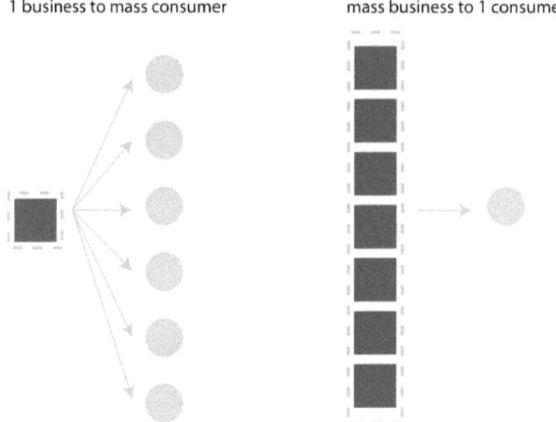

Traditional mass consumer market, imply that we would have a unique offer that would be distributed to a large amount of consumers. The N=1, R=G present the opposite approach where businesses jointly help the consumer in the co-creation process of its offer.

It is the case of ICICI Prudential in India or Norwich Union in the U.K. to take an example of Krishnan, *"They're making health and auto insurance policies more flexible. The premiums you pay in these policies are based on your real-time behaviour. Auto insurance premiums are determined by where you drive and how you drive. Emerging technologies such as GPS tracking make it possible for firms to develop dynamic risk profiles."*

This take us to the interesting part of this demonstration which is "industry categorization & Embededdness of organization". In fact, the N=1, R=G complex the relationship between organisation that become at the same time highly diversified and personalized to capture the variety of needs of individual consumers. In the meantime all these organizations require a strong embededdness to deliver unique consumer personalized values. In the following we try to demonstrate the challenge associated to categorization and embededdness under the N=1, R=G model.

Industry categorization

We would consider industry categorization from a managerial perspective and the fact that it can be challenging for managers to work with other category of industry than their own. It is the reality and necessity of an N=1, R=G model that strength the use of resources that are not traditionally utilized by a specific industry. N=1, R=G tempt to force the relationship between industries of different walk. The history of innovation mentions plenty of situation for which firms were not able to adapt a particular change of technology or shift in society. Krishnan said: *"Several years back, Sony was very well known for Walkmans and personal music. This whole idea of listening to music while you're walking isn't new: Sony was on it long ago. What did Apple do? They changed the game. First, they digitized the content. They created a platform so you have your own playlist, your own podcast of content and news you want to listen."*

Firms are extensively bound to masteries knowledge which is traditionally not in their core strength to respond to the needs of the N=1, R=G model. As a consequence business loses their identity by embracing values that are not in their core strength. This loss of identity is often negatively felt by managers who have built their professional identity jointly with the identity of their organisation as a whole entity. Introducing new values and concept into the firm culture ultimately break established values. Rare are the companies who can systematically embrace new values and remodel their institutional identity to benefit from alternate business verticals. Managerial categorization of industries cost a lot to the innovation potential of an organisation. We have seen how Sony was not able to move towards digital technology. In positive moods managers may embrace new fields of research with a positive attitude towards other category of industry. However in time of struggle managers may have the tendency of stepping back to the industry they are familiar with. The shift from a traditional categorization of industry towards a flexible model N=1, R=G would force organization to destroy cultural barrier between industries.

Embededdness of organization

The N=1, R=G model imply a reinforcement of ties between organisation to respond consumer needs. Ultimately the reinforcement of ties could tempt to merge industry categories into a similar method of accessing values creation. The two fundamental changes that organisation embededdness would face are a reinforcement and mutation of ties. The reinforcement of ties is due to the alignment of organisations objectives towards a same goal which is defined by the user. The mutation of ties is due to the necessity for the organisation of repositioning itself within the cyber industry and creates new ties that are more beneficial to its prospective outlook.

Change management

Developing a new business culture represent the major managerial defy for companies to integrate participative innovation. The human aspects of this cultural change have been addressed previously. From a practical perspective 4 challenges have to be addressed to individual, teams and managers who participate to organizational change. They are the keys success factors to reach the successful shift towards an integrated system of participative innovation and social entrepreneurship.

Co-creative environment: Consumer involvement in the process of co-creation requires the development of tools to stimulate consumer entrepreneurship behaviour. Qualitative and quantitative research can support the profiling of individual to find personalized solution for social entrepreneurs.

Setting a new goal: To form new ties with other industries and benefit from the N=1, R=G concept. Firms need to set new goals that are outside their domain of expertise. This new goal shall respond to consumer/producer aspiration in terms of entrepreneurship role and leadership.

Measurement system: Organization would require new tools to measure consumer/producer success. Understand that, non-capitalistic values would be accounted as value creation for society. Various criteria like sustainability, Eco friendliness and social responsibility may be part of the assessment program of such organisation.

Systematic cybernetic: Crowdsourcing can contribute to the systematic profiling of consumer/producer, thus help them to connect with tools and platforms that contribute to their entrepreneurship project. Cybernetic is a strong aspect of N=1, R=G as no organisation is large enough today to develops the capacity of identifying opportunities without the help of technology. Internet has demonstrated to be powerful tools for market research. In the N=1, R=G system internet would be used to identify cloud opportunities.

Sequence of steps: In a *"prosumer"* economy understand, a co-created world. The industry remains an ongoing live testing of product and services. As product and services are tested they constantly come back to the industry for re-profiling. Solutions are partial and systemic, waiting for alternate solution to collaborate. Thus, the creative process of organisation is no more linear but cyclic. The sequence of steps for business creation is ongoing, what stress the importance of finding new systems of remuneration for organisation.

Research opportunity

Scholars in the field of sociology, design, business, and economy have debated the upcoming of a new type of socio-economic environment on which social entrepreneurship may take a major role under the impulsion of participative innovation. However, scholars in these fields have not yet adequately addressed the influence of one concept towards the other one. The conversion of passive consumer model into proactive model of social entrepreneurship could radically change the way businesses are conducted for corporate and social leadership. There is a strong gap in knowledge in the field of participative innovation and its influence on entrepreneurship. Academic and corporate efforts have only responded to the market need on surface without digging the ocean of possibilities offered by co-creation and social entrepreneurship. This gap is costing a lot to our economy; not only because there is a market opportunity which is untapped but also because our economy has been narrowed to the simplistic model of consumerism; cutting the way to any alternative opportunity of growth. The link between participative innovation and social entrepreneurship should be analysed in a sceptical way. However we hope that this research would bring light on the strength and weakness of such evolution of the social structure.

Research Design

This document paves the way to my research project. I am conscious that most of the elements presented are rudimentary and that extensive researches have to be made to furthermore understand the ecosystem we are working on. Therefore tools and techniques may be added or removed with respect to the ongoing research requirements.

The methodology here presented is chronological. It includes tools and process issue from 3 disciplines that are academic research, user research and design thinking.

Literature review to understand what has already been done, tested and understood in the field of Co-creation, Design Thinking, Business, Innovation, Social entrepreneurship, Cybernetics, crowdsourcing and Complexity.

User research would be used to gather insights directly from entrepreneurs and social entrepreneurs. But also 'common man' within the society who could with my reasoning becoming the design think-tank of the planet.

Design thinking itself would provide insights to draw new scenario in which design thinking would be used. Design thinking would also be used to elaborate the blueprint of a co-creative approach of social entrepreneurship.

Methodological process:

1. **Stakeholders' interview**

The research requires that we understand the environment of the subject we are working on. Literature review maybe a source of information, thus I believe that the entrepreneurship ecosystem should be understood at source with the current and potential entrepreneurs. The stakeholders interview must include all the protagonists who have an entrepreneurial activity but also those who deal and interact with them. This first phase of the project would be purposely 'fuzzy' in terms of information gathering has we must be open to surprizing findings that could be determining for the future of the research.

2. **Affordance mapping**

Information gathering from stakeholders interview and literature review must be organised in an affordance mapping that would help further to make relationship between clusters of informations.

3. **Quantitative research**

The primarily purpose of quantitative analysis is not to find data to aliment the research finding but validate that the subjects we are working on are of sizable importance for the research potential. The affordance mapping would be a source to isolate concepts that need to be presented with quantitative data. The further usage of such data will need to be addressed in point 11. Quantitative research may open the door to new areas of exploration that would be investigated through interview and literature review. The objective of this quantitative research is to question the completeness of the affordance mapping.

4. Study focus

The affordance mapping would be reviewed by the focus group to find potential research direction. The focus group would be run with entrepreneurs and potential entrepreneurs, thereafter compared with a panel of researchers for the same exercise. That dual experiment would allow us to understand the difference of appreciation between entrepreneurs and academician who may have a different standpoint. Both have their relevance for the making of the research. In the eventuality of large gaps of interpretation, those gaps could be explored furthermore to understand key issues in terms of socio economical understanding and interpretation of entrepreneurial concepts.

5. Socio type mapping

As the research has an inclination towards the understanding of the social role of participative innovation. It seems important to me to study the individuals that stimulate the social entrepreneurial culture. We are narrowing the study not to the entrepreneurial cells as an entity but to the individuals that compose it. Single individuals would be studied and grouped into socio types. Visual mapping may be used isolate socio-style and describe their function and identity within a given environment. That technic would also generate interesting insights for the making of the Persona and the development of the qualitative research.

6. Persona

Persona is a design technique that allows practitioners to visualize the role of a socio type in the usage of a product or a service. The benefits of such technique have been used by policy makers to represent social scenario with various protagonist. Our aim is to discover the major persona of the social entrepreneurship ecosystem and visualize the nature of links of their interaction. It is still not know if persona would have to be classified by the nature of their function of by social outlook.

7. Interview Preparation

Stakeholder's interview would be designed in such way that they reveal functional and cognitive insights from the selected personas. Open question would be preferred with lots of interaction space for the interviewed to reveal qualitative data. The interview preparation would include the making of a large social trends sample that would be presented to the interviewed for comment.

8. Interview

The interviews need to be conducted by the interviewer with the help of a moderator and eventual translator. The duration of a qualitative interview can vary widely from 30 min to 2.5 hours. The quality of an interview cannot be justified by time but by the relevance of its insights.

9. Observation

Observation allow researcher to make the difference between interviewee behaviour and attitude which is a fundamental insight of qualitative research. Conducting stakeholder's observation can be quiet challenging as they may be reluctant to share part of their activity. However this aspect of user research if often the most insightful as it reveal opportunities and challenges that are usually not shared during interview.

10. Validation technique

Most of the time validation technique would not provide additional insights to the interview. It allow just to validate that the gathered insight are correct and in accordance with the candidate preference. However, sometimes the interviewee preferences from social insight samples are very much different from

11. Quantitative validation

As we have said before the quantitative analysis can help us in understanding if the quality sample analysed is relevant of a significant population. Early quantitative data should be confronted to the collected finding of the interview to see if there is any conflict of information or more importantly any segment of the stakeholder that would have been neglected. Qualitative validation would be conducted in an intuitive way by comparing group of quantitative and qualitative insights. We will draw information relationship to isolate question and/or lack of information in both the side.

12. Literature review

The research must be integrated into existing content produced by other research. Literature review in the particular domain of studies would help in isolating areas of development for the research. The literature review must be organized by domain of research (sociology, design, economic, etc.) Mind mapping offer a quick and meaning full representation of research area and opportunities.

13. GAP analysis

There is several ways to point a research gap and not given process. A research gap may highlight the fact that researches are incomplete in a particular area. Research may also be inadequate because not immediately linked to the phenomenon we want to study. Present research could be incommensurate or outdated. Several facts may have change the scenario making theories irrelevant. Another way to isolate research gap is to look into contradictory facts that could have been due to lack of knowledge of sampling error. A research gap can be built on the fact that research want to open a new field of development and need theories to develop future research. Limitations can be a way of justifying future research by building on existing studies and findings. Identifying the research gap in this stage of the project development is essential to optimize the exploitation of the wall affinity diagram that follows.

14. Wall affinity diagram

This technique consist in visualizing research insights to draw relationship between the groups of information and build ether a research paper or a business scenario on which stakeholders would play different roles. The major contribution provided by this tool is the fact that insights would become available for the whole research team. Beside this participants from various background (psychology, IT, etc.) can easily find their way through the flow of information and draw meaningful conclusions that can be compiled together to design ether a research paper or a business scenario.

15. Scenario making (optional)

Scenario is most of the time utilised by designer to understand social relationship around a particular product or service. It the case of academic research the scenario may not have a strong relevance to justify theories and facts. However the scenario can help the researcher by providing contextual insights to the research. A scenario always include persona that are rich of information to justify research finding with appropriate examples. The scenario can surely help the research is giving 'life' to the research finding.

16. Narrative demonstrative (optional)

Narrative could be an option to illustrate research finding into hypothetical scenarios by going through the stakeholder's experience. The narrative has the advantage of connecting disparate insights into a coherent scenario. Bring sense to hypothetical findings that could have not been highlighted using another format. The narrative like the scenario making is one of the options to present the research findings.

17. Theory building (optional)

The research would ultimately lead to theoretical finding that can be tested back with the stakeholders to validate its foundation. Once validated theoretical finding can be explain with examples. Research gap analysis would therefore play a major role in opening the platform for new theoretical building.

The research design would be a combination of the several experiment presented here above. The aim of this research is to demonstrate the relationship between participative innovation and social entrepreneurship. Both subjects will be developed separately before presenting the links between the two. From an overall perspective the idea is to build on the shoulders of giants while opening new research opportunities for the future.

Conclusion

I expect this research to contribute to the debate on participative innovation and social entrepreneurship that I assume to be linked. I attempt to understand the relationship between both happenings and analyse how organization are at risk of been bound in changing their innovation strategy towards a participative approach. I wish to prove the eventuality of a *"do-or-die"* theory that would force corporations in promotion a rearrangement of the society towards social entrepreneurship. I may be able to demonstrate that business and society are at risk of having to give-up the command of the politic, economy and industry to the common man. On the other hand, balance should be given and I may be able to demonstrate that going towards such direction open new opportunities for both the end; business and society.

Reference

Anderson, C. 2012. La Longue Traîne : Quand vendre moins, c'est vendre plus. Makers : La nouvelle révolution industrielle.

Bauman, Z. 2000. The Individualized Society. Cambridge : Polity.

Eychenne, F. 2012. Fab Lab : L'avant-garde de la nouvelle révolution industrielle.

Holmgren, D. 2002. Permaculture: Principles & Pathways Beyond Sustainability.

Howe, J. 2009. Crowdsourcing: Why the Power of the Crowd Is Driving the Future of Business.

Nussbaum, B. 2011. Design thinking is a failed experiment – So what's next? Retrieved on May 7, 2013 at http://www.fastcodesign.com/1663558/design-thinking-is-afailedexperiment-so-whats-next.

Paitra, J. 2000. La société de l'autonomie, Comment les comportements vont changer.

Prahalad and Krishnan, 2008. The New Age of Innovation: Driving Cocreated Value Through Global Networks.

Kaufmann, J.-C. 2004. L'Invention de soi. Une théorie de l'identité. Paris : Armand Colin.

Roth, S. 2014. Fashionable Functions. A Google Ngram View of Trends in Functional Differentiation International Journal of Technology and Human Interaction 10(2), forthcoming

Surowiecki, J. 2005. The Wisdom of Crowds.

Roth, S., Kaivo-oja, J. and Hirschmann, T. 2013. Smart Regions. Two Cases of Crowdsourcing for Regional Development, International Journal of Entrepreneurship and Small Business 20(3), 272-285.

Roth, S. (2009), New for whom? Initial images from the social dimension of innovation, International Journal of Innovation and Sustainable Development 4(4), 231-252.